THEN & NOW

BERWYN HEIGHTS

THEN & NOW

BERWYN HEIGHTS

Ann Harris Davidson

For Stephen White, my love and support,
and Imogen Davidson White, our daughter and an inspiration.

ISBN 978-0-7385-5367-2

Library of Congress control number: 2007939189

Published by Arcadia Publishing
Charleston SC, Chicago IL, Portsmouth NH, San Francisco CA

Printed in the United States of America

For all general information contact Arcadia Publishing at:
Telephone 843-853-2070
Fax 843-853-0044
E-mail sales@arcadiapublishing.com
For customer service and orders:
Toll-Free 1-888-313-2665

Visit us on the Internet at www.arcadiapublishing.com

ON THE FRONT COVER: Elizabeth "Libbie" Stoner was the first owner of the 1888 home at 5717 Ruatan Street. Page 2 of the *Washington Post* of July 24, 1886, reported that Stoner had worked for the U.S. Treasury Department for more than a quarter of a century. She had been among the first women appointed to work for the U.S. government in 1862, when Gen. Francis E. Spinner, the treasurer of the United States, decided that women could trim currency faster and better than men and for half the pay, while the men were needed as troops in the Civil War. (1928 image courtesy Joseph R. Chlopicki; 2004 image courtesy M. David Williams.)

ON THE BACK COVER: After a few years of renting this two-acre property in Berwyn Heights, Joseph V. and Vladislawa "Gladys" Chlopicki bought it in 1928, and then established a 2,000-chicken farm where Joseph (left) and a worker were photographed. Though no longer a farm, the house (far left) with a one-acre yard still belongs to the family. (*C.* 1930 image courtesy Joseph R. Chlopicki.)

Contents

Acknowledgments

Thank you to the many former and current residents of Berwyn Heights who shared their photographs, memories, and knowledge of life in Berwyn Heights with graciousness and joy. Individuals searched their attics and albums for useful images and helpfully suggested other people to approach. The keen memories of Mary Louise Milstead, Jean McConnell, Ruth Ellsworth, Elizabeth Prosise, Mary Louise Snidow, Maria Snoddy, Edna Waters, and Lucile Dwiggins made Berwyn Heights of 50 to 80 years ago come alive and, with their donations of photographs, made producing this book possible. Frances Keefauver Hoyert enriched the information on the religious, commercial, and social overlaps between the Berwyn Heights and Berwyn communities.

Other individuals who provided images, sometimes posting them from elsewhere in the United States, include: William Abrams; Oscar Agee; William A. Aleshire; Jerome Anzulovic; Raymond W. Bellamy Jr.; E. C. Carrington VII; Jane Chick; Joseph R. Chlopicki; the Cicotte family; James Demino; the Carl Gohr Jr. family; Paulette Wintermoyer Gould; Cooper Graham; Albert B. and Blanche Hill; Anthony Holmes; June Johnson; the Lofgren family; the Morrow family; Janice Neilson; Edwin Waugh Ronsaville III; Rita Sayer; Shirley Sorensen; Georgina Stark; Carole Waesche; M. David Williams; the Woods Vignola family; and Elizabeth Zinecker.

Organizations that provided images and their representatives, who made their use possible and who sometimes helped to frame the modern images, include: the Berwyn Heights Volunteer Fire Department (James Woodhouse, Chief Charles Fusco, and crew); the Berwyn Heights Town Office (Kerstin Harper and Darlene Erickson); the Berwyn Heights Police Department (Chief Patrick Murphy); the Berwyn Heights Elementary School (Dr. Karen Singer, Sharon Cook, and Darelynn Fung); the Berwyn Presbyterian Church (Rev. Dr. Renée Mackey); the University of Maryland Libraries (Douglas McElrath, Patricia Cossard, Cindy Larimer, and Gail Rumper); My Eye Dr. (Drs. Norman Fine, Beverly Miller, and Charles Mund); Giant Food (Jamie Miller and Sgt. Richard Hartnett); the Daughters of the American Revolution (Tracy Robinson); the Prince George's County Historical Society (Susan Pearl); the Maryland State Archives (Christopher Kintzel); and the Historical Society of Washington (Yvonne Carignan).

Throughout the book, all now images are courtesy of Ann Harris Davidson unless otherwise noted.

References

Burch, T. Raymond. *History and Development of the City of College Park, Berwyn Heights, Greenbelt and Adjacent Areas*. College Park, MD: City of College Park, 1965.

Skarda, D. D. *Berwyn Heights: History of a Small Maryland Town*. Berwyn Heights, MD: Bicentennial Project, Town of Berwyn Heights, MD, 1976

Prince George's County Land Records.

The *Washington Post*.

INTRODUCTION

Small in size and population and often overlooked for being nestled between two larger, newer, and better-known cities, it is easy to understand why Berwyn Heights and its history are little known outside the town. It is a town of contrasts. It is a small town that lies within a big city, being part of the inner metropolitan area of Washington, D.C. It was designed as a carefully planned residential development for the elite of Washington, but it grew sporadically and in ways not planned. It is the sixth oldest municipality in Prince George's County, but 93 of Maryland's 157 municipalities are older than Berwyn Heights. It is not as it was, not even in name, but continues to engender the devotion of many of its residents. This volume weaves the past with the present to expose some of these contradictions while sharing its richness and consistency.

Berwyn Heights received its charter as an incorporated municipality from the Maryland General Assembly on April 2, 1896, but, in the eight preceding years, it had been Charlton Heights. Personal relationships and events explain why the name Charlton was originally selected and why it was not maintained. Benjamin Charlton was a wealthy and prominent Washington businessman who had inherited the successful Havenner's Bakery from his father-in-law and who was a trustee of the "Church of Presidents," the Metropolitan Methodist Episcopal Church. His nephew, Edward Graves, worked with him at Havenner's. Towards the end of 1887, Graves had made two purchases of land totaling 393 acres in Prince George's County just east of the Washington Branch of the Baltimore and Ohio Railroad. By mid-1888, Graves had had the entire "Graves' Subdivision" platted for residential development and had named it for his benefactor. Then Graves, with Charlton, James E. Waugh (from whom Graves had bought the southern 146 acres of the subdivision), and three other prominent Washingtonians incorporated the Charlton Heights Improvement Company, which immediately purchased the 393-acre subdivision.

Sales remained slow despite the effort to promote the development as an elegant address and a sound investment. By 1890, Waugh had formed a new group, the Charlton Heights Investment and Building Association, of which Charlton and Graves were not members, and he launched a campaign to divide Prince George's County into two, with the new county formed from the northern half and having Charlton Heights as its seat. Substantial promises were made, including that a courthouse and a grand hotel would be built, with the hotel costing $100,000 and having all modern improvements, including baths, electric lights, and elevators.

Some development did occur. The public Pine Grove Academy opened in 1889. Investors and residents funded the construction of the Charlton Heights railroad station building. About 20 Victorian homes, many of them designs from R. W. Shoppell's Cooperative Building Plan Association, were built in Charlton Heights. The cornerstone for a grand new church was laid on May 18, 1890, with the church completed and dedicated as the Charlton Heights Mission on April Fool's Day, 1891.

The push to divide the county failed, perhaps because its suggested name was Lee County, after Gen. Robert E. Lee. The promised hotel and courthouse were not built. The flattering articles that had appeared in the *Washington Post* in 1890 ended. Real estate sales did not improve. Worse, new articles appeared, this time concerning lawsuits from disgruntled investors. The Charlton Heights Improvement Company failed in 1892.

Immediately following the dedication of the Charlton Heights Mission, Frank L. Middleton, who, with his brother and father, had been instrumental in establishing and building the church, requested that its name be changed to Berwyn Chapel in honor of a friend who was from the Berwyn area on the Philadelphia Main Line, which had been settled by Welsh immigrants, and who had given a substantial donation in the name of his only son, an invalid. The congregation agreed to the change. Shortly thereafter, Middleton and other residents are said to have asked the Baltimore and Ohio Railroad to change the name of the station from Charlton Heights to Berwyn. This request was also granted.

The area west of the railroad station changed its named from Central Heights to Berwyn to match the church and the station. Benjamin Charlton died in 1894. James E. Waugh died at his home in Charlton Heights in 1895, and Edward Graves sold his home in Charlton Heights to St. Joseph's Union (which would use it as the St. Ann's Infant Asylum summer home) to focus his attention on the bakery business he had inherited upon his uncle's death. When residents of Charlton Heights, including John J. Kleiner, a former Democratic congressman from Indiana, petitioned the Maryland General Assembly for incorporation as a town, it was in the name of Berwyn Heights. Thus Charlton Heights became Berwyn Heights in 1896.

Though the incorporation was only of Berwyn Heights (east of the railroad), the administrative division did not reduce the collaboration between Berwyn and Berwyn Heights, especially as the railway station, post office, a church, and the fuel and grocery stores were all on the Berwyn side of the tracks. The later closing of the road over the railway tracks at Berwyn Road was deeply resented and did divide the two communities, though they continue to share the Berwyn Presbyterian Church, which is now back in Berwyn Heights, and Holy Redeemer Catholic Church in Berwyn.

Farms, notably with chickens, were established in what had been intended to be an upscale residential development. Development proceeded erratically, with each new round characterized by a different style of house, leading to Berwyn Heights having a chronological smorgasbord of homes that reflect popular American housing trends. There are wood-framed Victorians, early-20th-century four-squares, and 1920s bungalows, which were followed by brick Cape Cods and ranch homes before the boom of the ramblers that were built between the mid-1950s and the mid-1960s.

Irrespective of the changing styles of housing, or of the sports played by the children, each generation of residents has put a priority on having good public elementary schools. In cycles over decades, residents have protested the removal of teachers, petitioned for larger and better school facilities, testified at public meetings, conducted censuses of the town, and lobbied their elected representatives to have schools built or reopened. Similarly, the volunteer fire company has served the town since before it elected its own local government officials and has continuously provided valuable services.

That it has been possible to photograph so many family members then and now, a half to three-quarters of a century later, confirms their loyalty to Berwyn Heights. There are residents who have lived here 75 years and more and others whose families have seen up to six generations live here since 1896. This record is in part an homage to these people, along with an introduction to others of some of the rich history of what might, at brief glance, appear to be a nondescript little town. It is an invitation to enjoy the streets of Berwyn Heights, as seen through different eyes.

Author Ann Harris Davidson would like the collection of historical images of Berwyn Heights to expand and encourages readers to offer their photographs at ahdavidson@verizon.net or at 301-345-1624.

CHAPTER 1

Charlton Heights

James E. Waugh was a prominent Washingtonian and a Knights Templar eminent commander. By 1887, notable city businessmen were investing in land in Maryland. In 1888, Waugh, Edward Graves, Graves's uncle Benjamin Charlton, and three others incorporated the Charlton Heights Improvement Company, then purchased 393 platted acres from Graves. And so began Charlton Heights. (1876 image courtesy Edwin Waugh Ronsaville III.)

In the late 19th century, R. W. Shoppell's Cooperative Building Plan Association offered pattern-book plans for houses. The Charlton Heights Improvement Company built a handful of Shoppell homes in Charlton Heights, as Berwyn Heights was named until 1896, thus giving Berwyn Heights the best collection of Shoppell homes in Prince George's County. Shoppell Design No. 216 at 5804 Ruatan Street is on the National Register of Historic Places. It is known as the O'Dea House for the family who owned it for six decades from 1939. In 1960, Alice O'Dea became the first woman to serve as a Berwyn Heights' commissioner. (R. W. Shoppell, *Modern Houses*, 1890, page 134, courtesy the University of Maryland Libraries.)

James E. Waugh selected a prime location for his home, Edgewood, on the crest of the hill at the eastern edge of Charlton Heights. Waugh eschewed the Shoppell pattern-book designs; he hired a renowned Washington, D.C., architect, Thomas Schneider, to design his home, though the home may not have been built as designed. A later owner, blind Sen. Thomas D. Schall, called it Wyncrest when he represented Minnesota in the U.S. Congress from 1915 to his death after being struck by a car in 1935. By 1959, a developer owned the property. He removed the swimming pool, the tennis court, the stables, and the lodge; allowed the Berwyn Heights Volunteer Fire Department to burn down the mansion; then built 14 homes. (Historic image, private portfolio of T. F Schneider, courtesy Jerome Anzulovic.)

Modes of transportation and much else have changed since the Waters family owned Sportland, now at 5933 Natasha Drive, early in the 20th century. In the 18th century, it had formed part of Archibald Edmonston's 1,600-plus-acre estate, Yarrow, and it was known as Carrington's Farm from 1869 to 1903 when owned by General Carrington and his family. Part of the house dates back to 1790, making it the oldest home in Berwyn Heights and the only remaining structure that predates the 1888 formation of Charlton Heights. Stories and legends abound about this old home and its occupants. (1918 image courtesy the Waters Snoddy family.)

Edward C. Carrington II was born in Virginia in 1825. He organized the Richmond Rangers, the first company to offer its services to the government in the Mexican war. President Buchanan commissioned him as a brigadier general of the District Militia. President Lincoln appointed him as the U.S. Attorney for the District of Columbia, in which capacity he also served Presidents Johnson and Grant. General Carrington retired to his newly acquired country property, Sportland, in 1869, nearly 20 years before the creation of Charlton Heights surrounding his land. A direct descendant, Edward C. Carrington VII, is today a scholar-athlete at one of the nation's most prestigious universities. (1861 image courtesy the Historical Society of Washington and Cooper Graham; current image courtesy the Carrington family.)

The home at 5717 Ruatan Street shares characteristics with other historic homes in Berwyn Heights: it is a Shoppell design (No. 449) and a woman first owned it. In 1888, Elizabeth Stoner bought it as an investment, renting it while paying back the $2,500 she borrowed, then selling it in 1903. From 1923, Polish-born Joseph Chlopicki (a descendent of Gen. Joseph Chlopicki, Poland's leader in 1830) and his Russian wife lived here, buying the home and surrounding eight lots in 1928. More than eight decades later, their son still lives here; no other home in the town has belonged to one family for so long. (R.W. Shoppell, *Modern Houses*, 1887, page 8, courtesy University of Maryland Libraries, Special Collections.)

This 1888 house, now at 5712 Ruatan Street, may be a variant of Shoppell design No. 204. Subsequent to the historic photograph, a second story was added on its east (right) side. Jean Brelsford, whose parents moved to Berwyn Heights before 1900, bought it in 1923 and sold it to Carl Gohr Sr. in 1950. Carl Gohr Jr. has owned this home since 1962. A fourth-generation member of the Brelsford family, a granddaughter of Jean Brelsford, still lives on Ruatan Street, giving her family nearly 110 years of continuous residence in Berwyn Heights. (1910 image courtesy the Gohr family.)

Ernestine Studley bought 12 lots from the Charlton Heights Improvement Company on the first day the company offered sales, October 15, 1888. Her house was Shoppell design No. 462, the most expensive offered by Shoppell's Cooperative Building Plan Association in 1887. By 1893, Studley had defaulted on her mortgage. She had earlier been indicted as Ernestine Becker for embezzlement for defrauding her employer, the U.S. Treasury Department. Helen "Nellie" Davidson Kleiner, the wife of John J. Kleiner, who had served Indiana as a congressman (1883–1887), bought the property in 1895. By 1947, when Nellie's surviving grandson sold it, the Kleiner family had owned this home for more than 50 years. (1890 image courtesy William Abrams.)

Eugenia Washington, who never married, bought this property from James E. Waugh in 1892, less than a year after she had been one of the principal founders of the Daughters of the American Revolution. She owned what is now 5706 Berwyn Road until her death in 1900. Her grandmother was Lucy Payne, the sister of Dolly Madison, the "Widow Todd" who had married President Madison in Harewood, the Virginia home of Eugenia's grandparents. Her grandfather was George Steptoe Washington, Pres. George Washington's favorite nephew, who received an inheritance from the childless president. (Historic image courtesy the National Society DAR.)

Richard and Carol Cissel have owned this beautiful 1889 home for more than two decades. Samuel Moyer and his family owned it for more than three decades when he was a solicitor for the U.S. Department of the Interior. Moyer was the first and longest-serving president of the Berwyn Heights Volunteer Fire Department (1924–1935) and was elected to the Berwyn Heights Town Council during the same period (1926–1936). A granddaughter who was born in this house, Jean McConnell, has owned her own home in the town since 1957 and is the long-serving president of the Berwyn Heights Seniors' Club. (1926 image courtesy Jean McConnell.)

A dozen articles promoting Charlton Heights appeared in the *Washington Post* in the summer of 1890. One, titled "Terraced Villa Sites: Panoramas Which Delight Residents of Charlton Heights," named the successful people who had already invested in Charlton Heights, saying, "Edward [*sic*] Cross, on Keleher Avenue, has a pretty residence which is fast nearing completion." Ebenezer Cross was the first owner of this pretty residence, now with 5805 Ruatan Street as its address, but, like many of the early properties, it was frequently rented until 1921, when the Klein family bought it. (1891 image courtesy the Woods Vignola family.)

FOR SALE—SUBURBAN PROPERTY.

FOR SALE OR EXCHANGE — AT Charlton Heights, Md., 1 11-room cottage, stable, and hennery, with 2 acres of ground beautifully laid out in lawns, terraces, and vegatable garden; all kinds of fruit now bearing, lovely flowers, concrete walks; house has all modern conveniences, including hot and cold water, tiled bathroom, hot water system of heating, stationary tubs and gas, concrete cellar, good well and cistern, magnificent scenery, high elevation; also 1 6 and 1 8-room house at a bargain; easy terms and R. R. tickets to parties wishing to look at property by applying at 474 C st. nw. or P. J. KELEHER, Charlton Heights, Md.

Washington Post, May 14, 1894, page 3

The Charlton Heights Improvement Company had built homes to market its suburban development, but the company failed within four years, leaving hundreds of lots unsold, along with about 11 houses the company had built. In 1892, Edward Graves bought back unsold houses at a cost of $40,000; this home, now at 8707 Sixty-second Avenue, was one of them. Peter J. Keleher lived in it and acted as Graves's real estate agent, placing advertisements in the *Washington Post*, such as this one on May 14, 1894. The address given in the advertisement, 474 C Street, NW, was the address of Havenner's Bakery, which Edward Graves inherited from his uncle, Benjamin Charlton.

The 1890 home at 5622 Ruatan Street is another one the Charlton Heights Improvement Company built but was unable to sell, leaving it rented for many years. The rare photographs of the development's earliest days show the land cleared of trees with few homes. Even with young trees and with picket or low fences, the town still had a sense of physical openness in 1910. Now, with more than 1,000 homes and with large trees on almost every lot, that sense of spaciousness has vanished. (1910 image courtesy Elizabeth Zinecker.)

This home, now at 5625 Ruatan Street, was also amongst those that the Charlton Heights Improvement Company was unable to sell before its collapse in 1892. Though the original plat of Charlton Heights showed streets with names, houses were identified by the names of the families who occupied them. Ruth and John Sauer bought this home in 1924 and owned it until 1981; thus it was known as the Sauer House. House numbers were of less significance until postal delivery to homes started after 1948. Until then, residents collected their mail from post office boxes at the Berwyn Post Office. (1928 image courtesy Ruth Ellsworth.)

The Keefauvers once owned several properties in Berwyn Heights, but they were known for their general merchandise store. From before the incorporation of Berwyn Heights in 1896 to the mid-20th century, residents collected their mail from the western side of the tracks in Berwyn. J. Fred Keefauver served as the postmaster from 1897 to 1914, and his wife, Minnie, did so from 1918 to 1934. Now, the postal service delivers mail to homes, there is post office service in the Berwyn Heights Town Office, and a store that sells uniforms occupies the location of the Keefauvers' store. (Historic image Frances Keefauver Hoyert.)

The Baltimore and Ohio Railroad (B&O) was the first to receive authorization from Congress to enter Washington, with the Washington Branch from Baltimore opening in 1835. In 1843, Samuel Morse won Congressional support for the installation of these telegraph lines and, in 1844, sent the first telegraph message in America ("What hath God wrought!") along them. In 1888, the B&O agreed to a stop at Charlton Heights on its western border, now in Berwyn, College Park, but the company would not fund the station; local residents financed the building at a cost of $7,000. The turreted 1890 building was torn down around 1962. Today the Metro Green Line runs parallel to these CSX freight tracks. (*C.* 1892 image courtesy Prince George's County Historical Society.)

CHAPTER 2

BECOMING BERWYN HEIGHTS

Charlton Heights Improvement Company's members campaigned in 1890 to divide Prince George's County, with Charlton Heights to be the seat of a new Lee County. The effort failed; sales remained sluggish. The company collapsed. The name of Charlton Heights was sullied, but the framework for it to become Berwyn Heights had been established. (1929 image courtesy Joseph R Chlopicki.)

Though lying within 10 miles of the White House, Berwyn Heights has a village atmosphere that has consistently inspired loyalty in its residents. Then and now, families have seen succeeding generations establish themselves in the town. Town resident Mary Louise Milstead is the youngest of Mabel and Frederick "Fred" Frost's children, six of whom were born in this house between 1917 and 1929, when the Frosts were its tenants and Fred was serving on the town's first board of commissioners. Mary Louise and her husband bought their own home in Berwyn Heights in 1953. (1917 image courtesy Mary Louise Milstead.)

This 1909 home was built at 8516 Fifty-eighth Avenue for Elwood J. Taylor during the second period of home construction in Berwyn Heights. Once there was an elegant pond in its south garden, with chicken coops and an orchard on the western parts of its land. Though it is nearly a century old, only two families have owned this home; its present owners, Darald and Sarah Lofgren, bought the property from the Taylor family in 1962. Taylor served 14 years (1926–1936, 1938–1942) as a town commissioner, and Darald G. Lofgren has served on the town council for 24 years since 1980. (1921 image courtesy the Lofgren family.)

On August 9, 1919, Berwyn Heights, Berwyn, Branchville, College Park, and Beltsville held a huge parade as a welcome home ceremony for World War I veterans. Berwyn Heights was not mentioned on the program, because the administrative division between Berwyn Heights and Berwyn was generally ignored with "Berwyn" covering both places. The parade started at the train station, entered Berwyn Heights on Waugh Avenue (Berwyn Road), then turned north along Huntley Avenue (Fifty-eighth Avenue) before returning to the station via Keleher Avenue (Ruatan Street) and continuing through Berwyn and Branchville. The annual Berwyn Heights Day parade on the first Saturday in May still features walkers, vehicles, and riders on horses. (1919 image courtesy Frances Keefauver Hoyert.)

John Waters, who owned a 13.75-acre property, built the open-air Sportland Arena, said to seat 4,000 spectators, and then formed the Sportland Heights Athletic Club on June 3, 1922, to promote commercial boxing matches. The arena was west of his home in a lower elevation and with access from Waugh Avenue (Berwyn Road). The first town ordinance concerned the issuing of paid licenses for recreational events, with the first license issued to Waters on June 23, 1924. Almost immediate protests from local citizens' associations that the "brutal contests" and associated activities devalued local properties caused the withdrawal of the licenses. Today the spot where Edward "Ned" Waters stood would be in the backyards of homes. (1924 image courtesy the Waters Snoddy family.)

Dr. Molyneux Laurence Turner and his family lived in this home in 1924, when the town's first board of commissioners appointed him as its first health officer. By the mid-20th century, Berwyn Heights' location within the Washington, D.C., Beltway resulted in a housing boom, with the rapid construction of smaller homes on smaller lots. The grand 1889 home at 5617 Ruatan Street that Robert Sadler McCeney photographed on June 6, 1909, is now so hemmed in by homes that it is no longer possible to photograph its side view, as Sadler McCeney did. (Historic image courtesy Maryland State Archives Special Collection MSA SC 1477-1-6373.)

Residents of Charlton Heights and then of Berwyn Heights usually worked in Washington, D.C. Town resident David Wade (left) worked as a trombonist in a theater orchestra in the District. Wade was a neighbor of the photographer Joseph V. Chlopicki, a Polish electrical engineer who worked as a projectionist in Keith's Theater on 15th Street. Today more residents work locally, such as at the nearby University of Maryland, at NASA's Goddard Space Flight Center, or elsewhere in the suburbs. Neighbor Elizabeth "Beth" Zinecker, being bid farewell by Joseph R. Chlopicki, works at the USDA's Beltsville Agricultural Research Center. (Historic image courtesy Joseph R. Chlopicki.)

Berwyn Heights underwent a third period of development in the 1920s with the construction of bungalows. Not since at least 1950 had owners of this bungalow at 8529 Fifty-eighth Avenue realized that it is a Sears, Roebuck mail order home; its current owners, the Davidson White family, rediscovered that it is the Argyle. Sears sold houses via its Modern Homes catalogs from 1908 to 1940. Materials were usually shipped by rail from the factory, with deliveries timed to allow orderly construction. The nearby Berwyn Station on the B&O enabled deliveries to Berwyn Heights. This home is the last remaining recognizable Sears house in the town. (*Sears' 1927 Honor Bilt Modern Homes*, page 106, courtesy Raymond W. Bellamy Jr.)

Most homes built in Berwyn Heights before 1930 had extensive yards with wells, windmills, ponds, garages, or sheds. The Morrow brothers joke with their photographer in the backyard of their home at 8529 Fifty-eighth Avenue in 1948, when that home had its garage, garden shed, and well; these three things no longer exist. A local contractor, William Casey, bought the rear third of both lots in 1959, demolished the garage and shed, and built another house. Other developers acquired the original home and its remaining land in 1968, had it re-platted into two triangular lots by surveyor Carl Gohr Sr., and squeezed a third house onto the original property. (Historic image courtesy the Morrow family.)

There were no public water mains in Berwyn Heights before the early 1930s; homes thus needed independent sources of water. Wells, water tanks, cisterns in the attics, windmills, and septic tanks were prevalent. This water tank was in the backyard of the house at 5712 Ruatan Street; it was removed after piped-in water was provided. Later the original sheds were removed; then, in 1996, a house with the address of 8802 Fifty-eighth Avenue was built on the cornfield. (1910 image courtesy the Gohr family.)

This intersection was of Avis Avenue and LaBelle Avenue, looking northeast over the Chlopickis' chicken farm to their house and barn. The same intersection is now where Quebec Street and Pontiac Street meet Fifty-seventh Avenue Lee Pryor, who is almost a member of the community for having delivered mail in Berwyn Heights since 1995, has just delivered to the eight homes that were built on the former farm. (C. 1934 image courtesy Joseph R. Chlopicki.)

Each new period of construction in Berwyn Heights has featured a different style of home. The fourth period, from about 1937, was of all-brick homes, one of the first of which was built at 6005 Pontiac Street by Henry Meyer. Paul and Shirley Sorensen bought this home in February 1946. More than 60 years later, Shirley, who is standing (left) in the doorway with her daughter, Ann, still owns and lives in this home. (1946 image courtesy Shirley Sorensen.)

The fifth period of home construction in Berwyn Heights mostly featured ranch houses built between 1948 and 1952. Examples of these homes are the Dwiggins House at 8608 Cunningham Drive and the Wintermoyer House at 5614 Ruatan Street. An exception was the stone-fronted home that William "Barks" and Louise Barkley completed at 6301 Tecumseh Place in 1948. The Barkleys built their home themselves; here Barks is creating the terraced landscaping on which Louise, still the home's owner and resident, stands 60 years later. (1947 image courtesy Louise Barkley.)

At least four houses in Berwyn Heights have been moved from their original locations. Three were moved between 1910 and 1915. Four homes (6200, 6202, 6204, and 6206 Seminole Street) that were built in the mid-1950s developed structural problems within 10 years from having water in their basements. All were sold in 1967 to become the south parking lot of the future Science Park office complex. The first three homes were burned down; the fourth was too close to the house at 6208 Seminole Street to be burned. The Barkley family bought it and had it moved to their property behind their Tecumseh Place home. (1967 image courtesy Louise Barkley.)

The Barkley family documented the move of the house at 6206 Seminole Street along three streets to 8807 Sixty-third Avenue. The move required an escort from the Berwyn Heights Police Department and the assistance of the local power and telephone companies to lift lines out of the way. The Barkleys' daughter, Susan Hunter, and her family still live in the home (left) on Sixty-third Avenue. (1967 image courtesy Louise Barkley.)

Most homes in Berwyn Heights were built in just over a decade, from the mid-1950s to the mid-1960s. In 1958, there was one house on this section of Quebec Place looking east from Sixty-second to Sixty-third Avenue. Like this one, most streets were then unpaved, rutted dirt. By 1967, the street was paved and lined with homes; it has remained essentially unchanged in the nearly four decades since. This rapid development in Berwyn Heights contributed to Prince George's County being identified as the fastest growing county in the nation in the mid-1960s. (1958 image courtesy Lucile Dwiggins.)

After the boom in the construction of small ramblers, the fashion in home design in Berwyn Heights became split-level homes, such as this one at 6009 Pontiac Street and others in the south of the town. Albert and Roberta Hill, who lived next door, built this home in 1967. By the 1990s, some old homes, such as the Sears home formerly at 5616-5618 Ruatan Street, were demolished to build two new homes. In the 21st century, the town has seen the first examples of older homes being torn down or built over to create larger single homes. (1967 image courtesy the Hill family.)

Edward Graves, a cofounder of Charlton Heights, chose a hilltop on which to build his home in 1888. In 1896, he sold it to St. Joseph's Union and its Sisters of Charity for use as the summer home for their St. Ann's Infant Asylum. The county board of education bought the once-grand home from the Sisters of Charity in December 1954. This photograph was one of the last taken before the vacant home was bulldozed prior to the opening of the new Berwyn Heights Elementary School. This St. Ann's lives on only in memories and in a few fragments saved by residents, such as the stone shown. (1958 image courtesy Lucile Dwiggins.)

CHAPTER 3

SCHOOLS AND CHURCHES

Miriam Farwell was a much-loved principal of the Berwyn Heights Elementary School. She served in that role in both the Ruatan Street and Pontiac Street schools for 20 years (1954–1974). The county closed the Berwyn Heights Elementary School in 1981; following its reopening in 2002, this portrait of her was again hung in the school. (Courtesy the Berwyn Heights Elementary School.)

The first public school in the local area, Pine Grove Academy, opened in 1889, appropriately in a pine grove just east of Charlton Heights, to serve that new development and the surrounding farms. Its teachers were responsible for teaching all subjects to all grade levels in a single room that had no running water and only a pot-bellied stove for heat. On September 5, 2007, Constance Belfiore, the head of the Friends Community School, stands in front of her environmentally friendly, straw-bale constructed school to welcome her students to their first full day in their new school near where Pine Grove Academy once stood. (1895 photograph courtesy the Waters Snoddy family.)

By 1920, the one-roomed Pine Grove Academy was inadequate to serve the growing population in Berwyn Heights. Parents petitioned the county public school system for a new school. For only $400, a resident of Berwyn Heights, John J. Kleiner Jr., sold 20,000 square feet on Keleher Avenue (Ruatan Street) to the Prince George's County Board of Education in 1921. The new two-room school was still under construction when its first students assembled on opening day; in the background, school officials tour the site. The white house in the background remains next to the former school but is now obscured by trees. (1922 image courtesy William A. Aleshire.)

Mary Culbertson was the first principal, with Kathryn Stein as her accompanying teacher, in the new two-room Berwyn Heights School. Grades one to three were taught in one room, with grades four to seven in the other. From 1925 to 1940, Emma Bowman was the principal. She lived in Berwyn Heights, first lodging with the Stein family, who lived in a large home between Waugh and Joyner Avenues (now at 5712 Goucher Drive). Later, she lived in a house on Fifty-eighth Avenue at Seminole Street. (1929 image by Emma Bowman courtesy Darlene Erickson.)

After World War II, the rapid expansion of the town's population outgrew its school, leaving the two-room school on Ruatan Street able to accommodate only the lower primary grades. Again residents of the town worked hard to persuade the county's board of education that the increasing number of children in town warranted a larger elementary school. The elementary school on Ruatan Street closed in 1958, at the time of the opening of the new Berwyn Heights Elementary School on Pontiac Street, but it continued as a kindergarten until 1973, when it was sold to the county government. Today it is a private home with a leafier view across the street. (Historic image courtesy Paulette Wintermoyer Gould.)

When the upper elementary grades could no longer be accommodated in the Berwyn Heights School on Ruatan Street, those students had to attend (without bus transportation) the larger Berwyn Elementary School in the Branchville area of College Park. The Branchville Volunteer Fire Company tore down the main part of the school soon after acquiring it from Prince George's County in 1994. All that remains of Berwyn Elementary is its rear single-story auditorium, which now serves as a storage annex for the fire company. (1954 image courtesy William A. Aleshire.)

The 1941 promotion of the grade seven class at Berwyn Elementary School was the first to be held in the auditorium addition to that school. Frances Keefauver of College Park (second from left, first row) and Mary Louise Frost of Berwyn Heights (third from right, second row) both still live in College Park and Berwyn Heights, respectively. The grade six class of 2007 was the fifth to be promoted from Berwyn Heights Elementary School on Pontiac Street after its 2002 reopening. (1941 image courtesy Mary Lou Milstead; 2007 image courtesy Oscar Agee.)

Construction of the new Berwyn Heights Elementary School was under way early in 1958. It opened in the fall with its enrollment exceeding its capacity. By 1962, a second wing had been added, parallel to the first, and joined by a breezeway to the original plan, as shown in John Baer's 1956 schematic design of the architects' plan. Another wing, to the southwest, was added in 1964. (1956 architectural design image courtesy the Davidson White family; 1958 image courtesy Lucile Dwiggins.)

Albert B. "Benny" and Blanche Hill posed in front of Benny's family home at 6007 Portiac Street shortly after their wedding in 1956. St. Ann's Summer Home for Infants is behind them. Benny's mother, Roberta Hill, had also grown up in Berwyn Heights, as she was the daughter of William and Margaret Willard, who had bought 5312 Quebec Street in 1909. St. Ann's was demolished in 1958, but it was not until 1974 that the Maryland–National Capital Park and Planning Commission constructed its community center. The planning commission has a joint-use agreement with the Berwyn Heights Elementary School that allows the school the use of the gymnasium. (1956 image courtesy the Hill and Snoddy families.)

In May 1971, the school held a clean-up day; its students happily gardened and removed trash. Exactly a decade later, in response to dramatically declining enrollments throughout the county's schools, precipitated both by the demographics of the baby-boomers moving through elementary school and by court-mandated race-based busing, which began in 1973, the board of education voted to close the school. The University of Maryland became the owners of the facility, using it as the headquarters for the Maryland Fire and Rescue Institute from 1987 to June 2001. (1971 and 2001 images courtesy Darlene Erickson.)

From 1996, residents of Berwyn Heights campaigned heavily for the return of the town's elementary school, conducting a door-to-door census to document the significant increases in the number of young children in the town and the high percentage attending private schools. Solid support from town, county, and state elected officials enabled funding for the relocation of the headquarters of the university's Maryland Fire and Rescue Institute and for the reconversion of the facility. The Berwyn Heights Elementary School, with another addition and a covered walkway, reopened its doors on Monday, August 26, 2002, once again with more students than it was designed to accommodate. (1971 image courtesy Darlene Erickson.)

The elementary school's front entrance served—and serves—as the locale for many of the school's activities. In 1961, Principal Miriam Farwell supervises her students' Halloween parade. Since reopening in 2002, the school has received about 150 students each day by bus from Riverdale Heights. As a part of modern safety and security procedures, Principal Karen Singer and her deputy, Sharon Cook, conduct yearly emergency bus evacuation drills. In the 2007 drill, Dr. Singer signals to an incoming bus to wait until all students have evacuated from the bus ahead. (1961 image courtesy Darlene Erickson.)

The community bonds between those in unincorporated Berwyn on the west side of the railroad and those in Berwyn Heights on the east were strong until the closure of their connecting road (Berwyn Road) in about 1942. Both sides of the tracks shared shops, the post office, churches, and social activities, which included the Berwyn Band (1898–1930). Today there is no adult community band, but the Berwyn Heights Elementary School has a specialty Music and Technology Program in which over 100 students take instrumental music classes; teacher Darelynn Fung (left) is seen here with some of her grade six students. (1914 image courtesy Frances Keefauver Hoyert.)

Until the late 1930s, Hyattsville High School served as the public high school for Berwyn Heights (with no bus transportation provided). Greenbelt High School was built in 1937 on the northern border of Berwyn Heights to serve both the new development of Greenbelt and the existing town of Berwyn Heights. Both high schools were later converted to junior high schools, then to middle schools. Parkdale High is now the town's assigned high school, though many attend the Science and Technology Program at Eleanor Roosevelt High School in Greenbelt. Berwyn Heights residents Ikumi Doucette (left), Emily Gehrels, and Joy Doucette (right) were members of Roosevelt's regional champion varsity soccer team in 2007. (Historic image courtesy Paulette Wintermoyer Gould.)

Gloria Walker of Berwyn Heights (standing third from the left) played on the girls' basketball team at Greenbelt High School in 1947–1948. Sixty years later, the school is no longer a high school, but it still serves the town of Berwyn Heights as Greenbelt Middle School and still fields a girls' basketball team, now coached by Ebony Hollingsworth. In 1947, only white students attended Greenbelt High School. Prince George's County Public Schools are now integrated. Maryland State Department of Education records for 2006–2007 show that Greenbelt Middle School's student population is 68 percent African American, 20 percent Hispanic, 6 percent white, and 6 percent Asian. (1948 image courtesy Carole Waesche.)

In 1874, the Reverend Samuel W. Haddaway organized the building of the first church in the area on an acre of land donated by the Jonathan T. Walker family. Named the Haddaway Chapel Methodist Episcopal Church to honor its founder, it was located off Branchville Road (now Greenbelt Road, between Sixtieth Avenue and Cunningham Drive in Berwyn Heights). Gen. Edward C. Carrington of the Sportland estate became a trustee. In the fall of 1907, the church accidentally burned down when the church janitor was burning leaves on the lot. Long after the church property had become a gas station, its tiny cemetery remained behind it, until it too was sold for commercial development. (Historical image courtesy Prince George's County Historical Society.)

After the fire in 1907, the Haddaway Chapel was rebuilt in Branchville in 1910, but its cemetery remained in Berwyn Heights. The Toaping Castle DAR Chapter compiled records on the cemetery in 1955. These showed that it had 27 plots, 19 of which were squares for six graves each, with Cora Lily Duvall, wife of John W. Duvall, interred there. Only 10 markers then remained, with the most recent being for John Bonnefond and wife, deceased in 1932 and 1920, respectively. Only that Bonnefond metal marker (front center) remained when the cemetery was deconsecrated in 1988. Disinterred bone fragments were placed together in a vault belonging to the College Park United Methodist Church on Rhode Island Avenue. (1988 image courtesy Jane Chick.)

The Charlton Heights Mission began at Haddaway Chapel in 1882 with a group called the Golden Chain that met at that chapel. In 1885, Golden Chain separated from Haddaway, affiliated itself with the Fourth Presbyterian Church of Washington, and built the Branchville Mission a year later. With rapid growth in Charlton Heights, a larger church was soon needed. The cornerstone for this Charlton Heights Mission was laid on May 18, 1890, just west of Charlton Heights, where Potomac and Quebec Streets now meet in Berwyn. Today only the former manse remains behind small brick homes. (1890 image courtesy the Berwyn Presbyterian Church.)

The sullied name of the Charlton Heights development caused Frank Middleton, a founder of the Golden Chain and of the Charlton Heights Mission, to request its renaming to Berwyn Mission in 1891, reportedly in honor of the late young son of a friend and church donor originally from the Welsh area of Berwyn on the Philadelphia Main Line. Many of the original residents of Berwyn Heights (including the Joyner sisters, the Brelsfords, and the Kleiners) were its congregants. By the late 1950s, the maintenance of the old building drove the Berwyn Presbyterians to build a new church, back in Berwyn Heights and once again the only church in town. (Historic image courtesy Prince George's County Historical Society.)

The Berwyn Presbyterian Church originally had separate devotional classes for men and for women, with a Miss Hunter leading the men's class in 1900. John Hall (back row center) lived on Seminole Street and was one of the young men of Berwyn Heights who was a member of the church and of this class. Now the church offers a mixed adult Sunday School class at its Greenbelt Road location. Gregory Bergren (third from right) has led this class since 2001. (1900 image courtesy the Berwyn Presbyterian Church.)

The Berwyn Mission formed a Ladies Aid Society in 1901 to support the church's work. Elsie Joyner (standing, third from left) led this women's group in 1925. The Joyner family farmed land in the area before the creation of Charlton Heights. Sisters Ada and Elsie Joyner had been amongst the founding members of the Haddaway Chapel in 1874 before joining the Berwyn Mission. Edward Graves named one of the original streets on his 1888 plat of the Charlton Heights subdivision Joyner Avenue (now Goucher Drive and part of Fifty-seventh Avenue) in honor of this family. Today's women continue their support of the church. (1925 image courtesy the Berwyn Presbyterian Church.)

The Berwyn Presbyterian Church came into being in 1914 when 142 members of the Berwyn Mission petitioned the Fourth Presbyterian Church of Washington, D.C., to become an independent church. The Fourth Church and the Presbytery granted the request. Its first congregational meeting as a Presbyterian church was held on May 18, 1914, with a young recent Princeton graduate, Rev. William A. Eisenberger, leading the service. Reverend Eisenberger resigned in March 1918 to be a chaplin during the Great War. In 2000, Rev. Dr. Renée Mackey, whose doctoral studies focused on multicultural liturgy, became the church's first female pastor. (Historic image courtesy the Berwyn Presbyterian Church.)

CHAPTER 4

A LOVED COMMUNITY

Berwyn Heights exemplifies the best of small-town America while being within a metropolis. Its volunteer fire department and other community groups play integral parts in its history and social fabric. In 1950, the volunteer firefighters fought a fire for hours. Lawrence J. O'Dea (in the cab) provided this photograph; Edward Grosskurth (third from left) still lives in Berwyn Heights.

The Berwyn Heights Volunteer Fire Department formed in 1924, following a split from the Branchville Volunteer Fire Company in the previous year when the apparatus was moved to a private property, Buffington's garage, in Berwyn Heights. As the 14th company inducted into the Prince George's County Volunteer Fireman's Association, its designation is Company 14. By December 30, 1930, when its official charter was approved, a firehouse had already been built on what is now Fifty-seventh Avenue. This second home housed two vehicles, including the 1928 Chevrolet chemical truck by which company president Samuel Moyer (third from right) and other charter members stood. The ladder truck, also on Fifty-seventh Avenue, highlights the changes in the size and sophistication of firefighting equipment. (1930 image courtesy Janice Neilson.)

The firehouse built in the 1920s on Avis Avenue (subsequently called Quebec Street and now Fifty-seventh Avenue) was originally single-storied. John Yost, whose 1925 Sears bungalow is at the left of the photograph, was the chief of the Berwyn Heights Volunteer Fire Department in 1931. The 1928 Chevrolet chemical truck (left) was still in service in 1950. Today a parking lot exit is where this firehouse once was, and the Yost House has had several additions, including one that extends towards the former location of the firehouse. (1950 image courtesy the Berwyn Heights Volunteer Fire Department.)

The Berwyn Heights Volunteer Fire Department bought a Diamond T fire truck in 1941, when Clinton D. Walker Sr. was the department's president. In 1929, Walker had been the second fire chief, after John Buffington. Membership in the department dropped during World War II, when the young men of Berwyn Heights served the nation. Walker again became its chief but, sadly, died after suffering a heart attack while fighting a brush fire on March 25, 1945. Chief Charles "Chuck" Fusco, seen standing by the 2006 Seagrave rescue squad with Shawn Dwyer at the wheel, has led the department since 2001. (1941 image courtesy Mary Louise Snidow.)

Nearby military installations operated aircraft during World War II, proving the need for special rescue units equipped to extricate pilots and drivers from crashed equipment. The Berwyn Heights Volunteer Fire Department formed the first Heavy Duty Rescue Squad in Prince George's County and one of the first on the East Coast in 1945. The 1950 GMC one-ton panel truck that was the department's second rescue vehicle is being used here in a water rescue training exercise. With Lake Artemesia less than half a mile from the station, the modern squad remains responsible for water rescues. (Historic image courtesy the Berwyn Heights Volunteer Fire Department.)

With the acquisition of the rescue truck, the double-bay firehouse was no longer large enough to accommodate all the fire and rescue vehicles. A triple-bay firehouse was completed on the property in 1953, but this served as the department's home for only 15 years. By the mid-1960s, the Springhill Lake and Beltway Plaza developments in western Greenbelt were factors in the drive to relocate the firehouse, culminating in its present location at Sixtieth Avenue and Seminole Street. The 1953 firehouse is now part of the Berwyn Heights Town Center, housing the Seniors' Club. (1953 image courtesy James Woodhouse, Berwyn Heights Volunteer Fire Department.)

Lined up in 1953 in front of what was the third home of the Berwyn Heights Volunteer Fire Department were (from left) the 1950 GMC paneled rescue squad truck, the 1939 Diamond T pumper with 500 gallon per minute capacity, and the 1953 American Marsh GMC 750 gallon per minute pumper. The department's fourth home was completed in July 1968. By 2007, the large vehicles included a 2003 Freightliner ambulance, a 2006 Seagrave rescue squad, a 1990 Pemfab rescue squad, and a 1992 Pemfab LTI ladder truck. (1953 image courtesy the Berwyn Heights Volunteer Fire Department.)

The young men of the town enlisted in the armed services in droves during World War II. Neri Clark, the son-in-law of John Yost, joined the navy. Sons of the Aleshire, Forrester, Frost, Kleiner, O'Dea, Walker, and Wiedel families were amongst the young men from a few dozen families in town who served in that war. John J. "Googie" Kleiner III joined the army, was killed in action in Normandy shortly after D-Day, and is buried in the American Cemetery in France. The local VFW Post 5627 is the Phillips-Kleiner Post, with Kleiner's name one of five on the World War II Memorial on Route 1. The Johnstone House, now owned by Jeannette Enderson, is behind Neri Clark. (1942 image courtesy June Todd Johnson.)

The "Air Raid Warden, Town Post" sign on Mary and Clinton Walker Sr.'s Pontiac Street house dates the photograph to World War II. It was the winter of 1943–1944 when cousins Mary Louise Kraskoc and Barbara "Bobbie" Walker played on a sled in the snow outside the home their grandparents had owned since 1925. Mary Louise's mother and Bobbie's father were two of the Walkers' 10 children. In addition to being a fire department volunteer during the war years, Walker was an air raid warden. More than 60 years later, Mary Louise is pictured sitting on the same sled. (Historic image courtesy Mary Louise Snidow.)

Charlton Heights had a boys' baseball team in 1894; the May 3, 1894, edition of the *Washington Post* recorded the team's 19-8 loss to Hyattsville's Junior Baseball Club. In 1958, a Boys Club started in Berwyn Heights with three baseball teams (Under-14, Under-12, and Under-10). The Under-14 team, coached by James McConnell, had only nine players. Now, as the Berwyn Heights' Boys and Girls Club, the town continues to field baseball teams along with several other sports teams. Edward Keane (standing, right) and Donald Cicotte (standing, center) coached the 2007 Under-14 baseball team. (1959 image courtesy Jean McConnell; current image courtesy the Cicotte family.)

The earliest recorded girls' sports team was the Berwyn Heights School's 1929 dodge-ball team. There is no longer a dodge-ball team, but the first all-girls soccer team was an Under-10 team that Ann Harris Davidson coached in the county's Boys and Girls Club leagues in 1997. By the Spring 2000 season, playing as Under-12, this team had a perfect 7-0 record, outscoring opponents 30-3 en route to capturing the county AA title with a 1-0 win over the Andrews Air Force Base Bullets. (1929 image by Emma Bowman, courtesy Darlene Erickson.)

In the late 1950s, Berwyn Heights created a squad of baton-twirling majorettes who performed in competitive events and in parades, as at the Greenbelt Labor Day Festival. Exactly when Berwyn Heights ceased to have majorettes is uncertain, but everyone remembers their vibrant pink uniforms. Berwyn Heights now has a memorable softball team. Under the coaching of James Demino, James Taylor, and Rebecca Horning (left), this team has a current 42-game winning streak, it has been the county AAA championship team for three consecutive years, and it has outscored its opponents 670-71. (1959 image courtesy Lucile Dwiggins; 2007 image courtesy James Taylor.)

Fashions come and go in recreational activities, as demonstrated by the lack of a squad of majorettes in the last quarter century. The Boys and Girls Club also no longer features a bowling team, as it did in the early 1960s when William Milstead (center) and four other boys posed with their trophies. Forty years ago, there were no recreational soccer teams for children in Berwyn Heights. Soccer is now a booming sport, with the club having around 100 children playing on various organized soccer teams. Stephen White was the coach of this boys' under-12 soccer team. (Historic image courtesy Mary Louise Milstead.)

Section Nine of the 1924 charter for the town of Berwyn Heights provided for the appointment of one or more bailiffs vested with "all powers of a constable of Prince George's County within the said town limits". By 1959, the town had a police force, which, with its newly created cadet force, is seen here standing with the town's safety commissioner, William Corcoran. Later the force was disbanded and then reestablished by 1976. In 2007, the town no longer has a cadet force but has eight full-time officers, including Chief Patrick Murphy, and has the lowest crime rate of any Washington, D.C., inner-Beltway area in Prince George's County. (Historic and current images courtesy the Berwyn Heights Police Department.)

The Berwyn Heights Police Department originally operated from the town office at 5600 Berwyn Road, including in a trailer behind the offices during their renovations. In 1998, the police department moved to rented premises at 5411 Berwyn Road. Chief Patrick Murphy and Officer Travis Young were at their current headquarters on the morning of October 2, 2007. (Historic image courtesy Darlene Erickson.)

Participants at the November 1919 Berwyn Heights Association meeting selected four lots at LaBelle Avenue (Fifty-seventh Avenue) and Waugh Avenue (Berwyn Road) as the location of the community home to be built by the association at a cost not to exceed $10,000. Three prominent residents and members of the association—Elwood Taylor, William Willard, and John McNitt—purchased the land on November 21, 1919, but the administrative offices were not built until decades later. Part of the existing town offices date from 1956, and there have been periodic renovations and expansions. As recently as 1991, there was no landscaping around the town center. (1991 image courtesy Darlene Erickson.)

The town center has undergone metamorphoses, changing to meet the changing needs of the community. The original administrative building is now under the low roof to the left of the addition that has the current front entrance to the town office. The building next door was built in 1953 as the home of the Berwyn Heights Volunteer Fire Department. Since 1968, at varying times, it has provided space for a teen drop-in center, for the former town library, for a computer room, and for the Seniors' Club. An elevator shaft was added in 1995 to make the upstairs multipurpose room more accessible. (Historic image courtesy Darlene Erickson.)

Margaret Benson was the first woman to run for the town's board of commissioners. She was unsuccessful in a 10-candidate contest in 1940 in which 113 out of 114 registered voters cast votes. Twenty years later, the voters of Berwyn Heights elected the first woman to the board when Alice O'Dea won office. O'Dea was reelected to a second two-year term, joining Kenneth Aurich, William Smith, George Lauterbach, and William Crawford in the May 1962 swearing-in ceremony. In May 2006, voters elected Darald Lofgren, Patricia Dennison, Cheye Calvo, Bradley Jewitt, and Jeffrey Gourley to the town council. (1962 image courtesy town clerk Kerstin Harper.)

CHAPTER 5

FACES AND PLACES

Winters might have seemed colder when Edward "Ned" Waters and his family lived at Sportland and had this view over Berwyn Heights. Waters established his own home in Berwyn Heights and later represented the area as its county commissioner (1950–1954). He died in 1965, but his widow, Edna, still lives in Berwyn Heights. (1917 image courtesy the Waters Snoddy family.)

In 1929, Edna Purdy married Edward J. "Ned" Waters, whose family had owned Sportland for nearly 15 years. Edna and Ned built their own home 100 yards from Sportland in 1933. Shortly thereafter, Edna was photographed with her daughter, Maria, and her neighbor, Annie Smith of 8515 Sixtieth Place. Seventy-three years later, Edna and Maria were photographed together, again with a neighbor (Zelda Bell) who has lived at 8515 Sixtieth Place for decades. Edna still lives in the home that she and Ned established, and at 97, in 2007, she is the oldest resident in Berwyn Heights. (1934 image courtesy the Waters Snoddy family.)

Well into the 1940s, there were farms with orchards, barns, cornfields, and chicken houses in Berwyn Heights. The Chlopicki family had a 2,000-chicken farm and a vegetable garden on the land they owned west of Huntley Avenue (Fifty-eighth Avenue) between Keleher Avenue (Ruatan Street) and Avis Avenue (Quebec Street) Gladys Chlopicki (right) and her sister, Rose, were photographed in the vegetable plot. Today the fields are a forest that neighbors Elizabeth Zinecker (right) and Ann Harris Davidson help Gladys's son to keep under control. (*C.* 1931 image courtesy Joseph R. Chlopicki; 2007 image courtesy Georgina Stark.)

Direct access from Berwyn Heights to the B&O Berwyn Railroad Station, to Route 1, and to the shops and post office in Berwyn (now in College Park) required crossing Indian Creek. The early-20th-century steel-framed bridge, with a planked surface on which Ruth Sauer stood in 1922, washed away in a flood. Maryland's State Highway Administration records that its concrete replacement was completed in 1933. Eighty-five years after she posed on the bridge, two of Ruth's daughters, Elizabeth "Bettie" Prosise of Berwyn Heights and Ruth Ellsworth of Silver Spring, stood on its replacement over Indian Creek. (1922 image courtesy Ruth Ellsworth.)

The 1933 concrete bridge over Indian Creek remains in service. Its once-grassy banks are now wooded. The road and bridge were a part of Route 434, which was a main automobile access route to U.S. Route 1 from the east. This road to the Berwyn area of College Park was closed at the railroad tracks, immediately west of the bridge, shortly after two Berwyn Heights residents, young teenagers William "Billy" Forrester and David Paul "Chick" Schniedman, were killed when a train struck their truck at the level crossing on April 18, 1942. (1938 image courtesy Ruth Ellsworth.)

Steep, terraced backyards in multiple small properties between Sixtieth Place and Sixtieth Avenue are remnants of a quarry. Its last use was to supply sand and gravel for the construction of Kenilworth Avenue. Neighbors Rita Miller of Sixtieth Place and Bonnie McCaw of Edmonston Avenue used it as a playground in the early 1950s, and 55 years later, Rita revisited the former quarry. In 1958, quarry owner Carl Jaeger Jr. sought a county permit to continue its use against the protests of residents of Berwyn Heights. The county commissioners unanimously refused the permit, leading to the land being sold for homes to be constructed starting in 1959. (1952 image courtesy Rita Sayer.)

The 1924 tax assessments recorded only a couple of small businesses; those taxed were McNamee Brothers Grocery Store and the Keefauver General Merchandise Store, both located on Berwyn Road near the railroad. The closing of Berwyn Road at the tracks and the rising dominance of motor vehicles led to businesses being clustered along Greenbelt Road. In 1976, Eye Associates, which became My Eye Dr. in 2007, converted a derelict gas station into an optometry office. Doctors and partners Norman Fine, Beverly Miller, and Charles Mund have been professional fixtures in the community since then, conducting their practice at the corner of Greenbelt Road and Fifty-eighth Avenue. (1976 image courtesy Dr. Beverly Miller.)

The McDonald's restaurant in Berwyn Heights was one of the first in the area when it opened in 1966. There were then fewer than 750 McDonald's restaurants in the entire country, with none outside the United States and none with drive-through service. As a student in high school, William "Bill" Milstead started working at McDonald's in May 1967, as soon as he was eligible to work. In the intervening 40 years, this local restaurant has remained successful, even with multiple other fast-food options now clustered nearby. Milstead successfully went on to other things, and the McDonald's has probably changed physically more than he has. (1966 image courtesy Mary Louise Milstead.)

Giant Food opened its store No. 83 at 8904 Sixty-second Avenue in Berwyn Heights on December 8, 1965. It was the first and only supermarket located in the town. By the early 1990s, Giant Food wanted a larger store to serve the area. On April 7, 1993, the company opened a bigger store across Greenbelt Road in the expanded Beltway Plaza in the city of Greenbelt, leaving its former premises to be occupied by Staples and Blockbuster Video. (Historic image courtesy Giant Food and Sgt. Richard Hartnett.)

The image of Wilton "Pete" and June Todd in their front yard evokes carefree summer days. They had reasons to be at ease as, from 1919, their maternal grandparents had lived a house away; their grandmother's brother built his house on this street in 1925; and three of their mother's sisters built their homes nearby in Berwyn Heights. Their grandfather, Mortimer Johnstone, and their great-uncle, John Yost, were two of the founders of the Berwyn Heights Volunteer Fire Department. Sixty-five years later, Pete and June revisited their former home, with an 1890 Prince George's County Historic Site still their backdrop. (1942 image courtesy June Todd Johnson.)

Branchville Road formed the northern border of Charlton Heights. The development of the city of Greenbelt to the north and east, led to the widening of the road, to a slight southern shift in its position, and to its renaming as State Route 193 (Greenbelt Road). By 1976, the Beltway Plaza existed immediately to its north, but the southern side in Berwyn Heights still had a bucolic feel. In 2007, the road is a heavily trafficked highway. With a connector road from Greenbelt Station developments planned here, the transition from rural to suburban to urban will be complete but, in spite of ongoing changes, Berwyn Heights expects to continue to be a wonderful place to live. (1976 image courtesy Dr. Beverly Miller.)

MAP SEARCH